JUST A THOUGHT

By

YOMI WILLIAMS

Published by New Generation Publishing in 2019

First Edition

www.newgeneration-publishing.com

*This book is dedicated to my children,
who I love with all my heart.*

Foreword

'Just a thought' is a collection of inspirational quotes from our brother. They are thought-provoking and provide insight to his gifted and creative mind.

Simi & Yemi

I have learnt that to know me, is to understand me. I have learnt that the most loving person, does not mean the most understanding person. The most caring person does not mean the right person. A miserable person does not mean a wicked person. A great personality does not mean a loveable person. But, two uneven people can make it work, effortlessly.

Just a thought

Yomi Williams

Contents

FAITH NUGGETS

- Exceeding *all* my expectations. You are the… Promise Keeper.
- In the world there is safety in numbers, but in the spiritual, there is safety in One.
- Then I was with him, the Master Craftsman. I was his delight daily, continuously rejoicing in his presence. The Word is My Word too.
- In order to see or feel the truth, one must be oblivious to, both your own and other people's opinion. The truth supersedes theory and opinions. It simply is "The Truth" and does not have to collaborate with your facts or findings. You have to search for the "Truth" and the truth is far from a "feel good" factor. It's simply The Truth.
- Attaching importance to anything does not mean you have control over the situation . Don't be fooled, even when you are in "control", it is only temporary. Control of anything is in He who holds your time only.
- I have learnt that when God keeps you alive, it's for a purpose, and he will open doors to the possibilities that you so long for. He who kept you alive, will not put you to shame. Remember, it is his plan, not yours, so why worry how it will materialise?
- Waking up every day is like, stepping into a boxing ring with your gloves permanently on, but if you trust in He who holds and controls your time, then the battle is not yours.

- You can't be angry with God and not believe in God at the same time, as both simultaneously feed off each other in agreement. Being angry does not eliminate love. As those that don't believe simply don't and blame logic, without involving the spiritual.
- A prayer is not meant for everyone to hear and gather "Amens", but simply for God to hear.
- The opposite of Life is not death…but Transition.
- Never be overly righteous, and if you are, remember one thing, He loved us first.
- Relax and let your spirit attain heights your body can only imagine. Let your Spirit stand tall in all things that weigh you down.
- Just because you are around danger, trouble, evil etc, does not mean you will be destroyed or burnt. Lightening is fearsome and I'm sure none in their right mind will like to be burnt by it, but can lightening run on ice? Put your trust in He who answereth by fire and destroys all sacrifices of evil.
- A release from the pressing issues of life, can be like breaking free from prison. It gets to a time when you are too stressed to deal with your own stress. Understand this, you are not born to solve all that life throws at you. Learn to cast your struggles unto He that holds your "time" in His palms.
- Men's heart failing them due to fear and for looking after things which are coming to earth. Despite love for materialism still, stress among both the youth and older generation, is at an alarming high. Let the Love and Joy of the Lord be your strength.

- Hear this: Circumcision that we follow has its benefits but was a covenant in the flesh. Those that didn't do it were "cut off" (spiritual disconnect/ disowned). True circumcision is in the spirit, which reconnects you back to the Father and prevails over everything, including the flesh that circumcision couldn't purge.

FRIENDSHIP NUGGETS

- The greatest gift you can give anyone, is to be by their side.
- Don't be fooled, a true friend does not need to tell you what you want to hear, but what you need to hear. Now that's having your best interest at heart. Only a companion need tell you what you want to hear, and if you are fine with that, it says a lot about you.
- Being surrounded by a pack of hungry wolves and expect not to be bitten or attacked is delusional. So, for those of you that hang around the wrong crowds and still complain about the stress you get from it, maybe it's time to change the circle you are in.
- When hidden dirt from your pasts gets drenched up, it could bury your hopes of happiness and trust, if it fails to be soaked up with understanding and forgiveness.
- Gift of Love: The greatest gift you can give anyone is to be by their side; not complaining, not stressing, but just being there.
- When things aren't going right, or when hard times rear its ugly head, very few folks will remain. Some folks will turn away – nothing wrong in that, but the most dangerous are those who "turn against" you, for no founded reason. Except for the fact that things aren't going right for you. In all remain unchanged. Not everyone is meant to understand your "race" or agree. But bless to those who standby regardless.

- The greatest Gift you can give anyone is to be by their side in thick and thin.
- The greatest gift you can give anyone is just being there.

HUMOUR NUGGETS

- Some people have serious negative energy, and yet they insist on meeting people with a sense of humour.
- God's Humour: For the righteous who think that God does not have a sense of humour. Ask the Israelites who ran around the wall of Jericho seven times for days.
- Woman Scorned: Man may have discovered fire, but women discovered how to play with it.
- Husband looked at wife and said, "I only have eyes for you" and wife replied, "That's all I ever get from you; your eyes".
- Due to the outrageous amount of debt owed globally, obscene pressure and manhunt to chase down debtors, a lot of people are meticulously faking their own deaths husband and wife will call a family meeting to decide who will die, how and when.
- When you put hunger before your self-respect, you are truly starving.
- Hmmm…the Israelites marched 7 times on the 7th day, round the wall of Jericho. That wall was 6 acres long…Ha. I would have fainted way before the miracle took place and been dragged away by a donkey.
- I'm only human, don't ask me for too much, too fast.

LIFE NUGGETS

- Our struggles, conquers and victory are bubbles we go through. Don't be fooled, all are entwined in our daily chapters.
- SILENT THOUGHTS: A lot goes on in silence and discreet in this head/mind of ours, but what would happen if we are judged for our guilty pleasures that go on in our mind? How many of us are locked up? How many of us will turn up in Church/Mosque, knowing that your secret thoughts have been watched? God has a reason for keeping certain things private, to preserve a degree of our dignity. So I say, some things are meant to be private/secret, not because they are bad, but just meant to be SILENT to the world. Let's face it, we do have enough issues than to bring secret thoughts into the light or public domain. If not, world issues will go into overload.
- Why spend most of your life satisfying your alter ego, and spend the rest denying and suppressing the better part of yours?
- Don't focus on self-defence as it comes naturally. The worst kind is self-denial. How do you reason with such a person?
- BEING YOU: Why spend a whole lifetime being what others want you to be; living for other people? What a waste of your God given talent. What a proverbial way of living that has got us nowhere. What about YOU!!! What makes YOU happy? What do you have to give to the world and most importantly, yourself? It's a waste of who you are,

and I don't mean euphemism. Most of all, no one accolades you for being who you are not, all you do is exhaust yourself and wake up one day, really sad, because the world didn't get to see what you had to offer as a human being.

- The reason why there is no cure for envy is because there is no cause for it in the first place. The individual who harbours envy is too self-absorbed with what others have, and never content with what they already have.
- MIDNIGHT CRISIS: Don't hate it when you go to the toilet in the middle of the night, and then you can't go back to sleep…Ha. It's almost a crime waking up to go to the toilet, with the fear of it breaking up a good night's sleep. Kissing my teeth.
- Double crisis is when you go into hospital due to cold, and come out with Jaundice, that's what seems to happen to quite a few folks. Go in with one thing and come out with another.
- Lingering doubts have a way of distorting progress.
- Don't be fooled as some people will rather die with a lie, than live with the truth exposed.
- Your goals don't put things into perspective. Reality and experience does. The consequences of both shape you.
- Nothing like "Alone Time"; it refreshes your nature.
- I have learnt that sometimes, it takes a problem to manifest in order for you to realise that you never

had a problem, when you thought you did. There are just present concerns.

- Don't be fooled. The righteous may be made right, but that doesn't mean you are right in things you do.
- A fool behind closed doors is better than one who displays ignorance in public with pride.
- You never see with your eyes because the truth lays within the mist.
- You are not defined by your success or failure, but you are sure redefined by trials and pressures of life.
- Be driven by passion not envy.
- Modern day era has given room to short term thinking.
- Body language always tells a different story, to what the mouth speaks. In reality the mouth speaks to disguise the heart; in secrecy, the heart speaks.
- The weirdest kind of people are those that have no boundaries, spend their time trying to be like others, write like others, say what others say. They have no sense of belonging, but want to belong to everything to create a façade of confidence or lack of it, in their case. Much easier being you. Give your inner self a sigh of relief by being you.
- A heavy mind and heart keeps sweet dreams at bay, and is a ton of weight around your ankles, hence making any kind of progress mute.
- Holding onto built up fear or anger is like a sneeze. It will inevitably come back more explosive than the first time you tried to hold on to it, bury it or

ignore. Your fear of moving on normally stems from the fear of letting yourself go, which does not entertain any form of progress. Letting go is always better than holding on.

- Everyone doubts an action or reaction we have committed. Afterall, we are Human and it is good to digest things at a later stage, and in most cases, you will get a more relaxed decision. Probably against your reaction. So there's nothing wrong in doubting what you doubted if reasons are now in the latter.
- I'm a simple person with a very complex nature. What truth in my irony.
- When you don't have freedom of choice on what's thrown at you, then there's no room for distractions on managing the risks.
- Searching for the truth in this modern era requires too much questioning before understanding - why bother, and it's a headache? It's much easier to follow and believe lies painted in deceit and wrapped up, in sweet and beautiful lies. Why won't it be easier, you don't have to do the thinking.
- The hardest thing to break is oneself and the hardest thing to face is yourself. But the easiest thing to do is criticise others. We are all fallible.
- Being indecisive or too complacent can be self-destructive and bring progress in anything , mute or stagnant.
- Would you lie to expose the truth? Or just let the truth simmer away in the wind until it reveals itself, as it will, because the truth will outlive our physical being. But waiting for the truth can cause a lot of

pain along the way and in some cases the consequences can be irreversible.

- It is hard for anyone to heal without answers.
- Self-esteem and self-confidence bring about a good balance of self-worth, but the lack of both is catastrophic.
- When Mankind are preoccupied with frivolities and mediocrity, they forget to appreciate what really matters, until chaos or a life changing situation strikes, and puts things in perspective. Then, what didn't matter is all that matters. Sometimes, it takes a problem to realise that you never had a problem, when you thought you did.
- If your decisions are based on bitterness and being vindictive, then you are ruled by it. There's a more refreshing life out there. Stop being clouded by bitter experiences because quite frankly, it does not change the price of fish and neither will it give you self-fulfilment.
- I have realised that you can never tell who will outlive you or be around the next second. How many times have you seen the frail and weak outlive the healthy and fit? We all take the luxury of time versus health for granted until a glimpse of reality rears its head and time stares us in the face.
- The best lies are smeared in half-truths to deflect the victim.
- What you think is good for you in your twenties maybe unreasonable in your thirties. When you get to your forties, you think, what was I thinking in my

thirties. In short – our thinking always evolves and metamorphose.

- It is amazing to have a mind of your own, as we all say, but a mind of your own isn't yours, if it's easily influenced or emotionally battered. It's the emotion that rules you then.
- I have learnt that when you think things can't get any worse, they sure can, but just as you think they can't get any better either; they sure can.
- Life is a constant battlefield, and in some cases you will be slam dunked with a sledge hammer back to Earth. The getting up sometimes seems impossible because we are overshadowed by the hurt, obstacle or issue to even foresee a solution. The difference between the impossible and possible is…Time.
- It is hard for anyone to heal without answers.
- When you look upon the face of a person and can't detect truth nor lies. You have a master of deception or Botox at its best.
- If you can master how to fake sincerity, anything else is a doodle.
- Life is not a problem to be solved, but a reality to be experienced. Live to learn.
- Grief always demands an answer, even when all ends are satisfactory.
- Sometimes folks fight tooth and nail to get out of the mess, they fought tooth and nail to get into.
- Don't be fooled, your understanding of the world cannot be fed or developed by the attributes and

contributions of mankind. The heart, mind and soul yearns for more and sees beyond the obvious, in other words, testifying to a higher self.

- Men's hearts are failing them for fear, and looking after those things which are coming on earth.
- Folks no longer aspire to excellence, but debased mediocrity.
- Everyone is pulling together and holding hands singing kumbaya, saying, 'we are not scared'. While in the shadows you can hear people whisper fears and watching where they tread…who is fooling who? Even the leaders have no satisfactory answers. Chaotic.
- Your inner spirit always wants to set you free from the cage of life's conforming attitude and expectations.
- Unresolved issues find a way of making opportunities knock.
- Most leaders of the world are doing anything but Lead.
- Assumptions are faulty or baseless until proven otherwise. You are none the wiser until you are informed.
- Misery and bitterness loves the company of those it detests. Never does it like standing alone, but its sole aim is to be contagious.
- I have learnt that we live in a world where we are not permitted without censure to follow our own thoughts in search of truth or the understanding of anything for that matter. The thirst for money and

wealth has overshadowed the zeal to acquire knowledge for self-development.

- Hmmm, sometimes we are so fast to get ourselves into trouble, but never fast enough to get out.
- Some folks are pushed to challenge themselves, whilst some simply challenge themselves. Either way, be fearless in challenging yourself.
- I have learnt that life imagined with experience can be re-imagined, and the life you defined with wisdom and experience can be redefined.
- Humans are beings that wear many masks, like layers of onions, all are revealed in due time.
- Amazing how we live among people who aren't people.
- Just make your mind up, or time will make it up for you.
- What are you surrounded by? What does the water around this boat represent in your life?
- Idleness sure gives room for frivolous gossip and itchy feet.
- Sometimes fear in itself creates a reason to be afraid. This stems from the anticipation of what we fear will materialise. The build-up of fear, could have more catastrophic effect, than the fearful event, itself, which may or may not take place.
- We don't move on in life because we need a reason to, but because we can and should. And whether you do or not, Time does not put itself on hold for you.

- A disingenuous life is always brought back to life, when reality hits.
- I can understand trying to fool others, but fooling yourself in the process – Delirious.
- No matter how focused or driven you are on chasing a project or desire, life always finds a way of throwing a preference you can't ignore. In short, it's a reminder you are not in control of things, even when you think you are.
- Complex in nature, we are, but the whole idea is to become less complicated as we age…well. for some of us… lol. Take pleasure in the simple things in life, given to us for free. Life becomes much easier when you stop caring what folks think about you. When you stop letting folks dictate what's in your best interest. Remember: Poor is the "Man", whose pleasures depend on the permission of another.
- A lovely environment does not set you up for a good night's sleep, but how you feel inside and what's going on around you does.
- Why are people titillated by what they cannot have? When they have it, the appreciation and hard work put into it evaporates. Are we discontent by nature? Or just driven by greed and materialism? Anyways, what's my own.
- Good memories will always have the pre-eminence over bad ones, the choice to let either rule is up to you
- How come kids question things but most adults don't…Hmmm.

- Lord, You make beautiful things out of dust.
- Who established the heavens? Who set the ocean boundaries, so that the water will not transgress it? Who marked out the foundations of the earth? Who was established from everlasting? Who made firm, the skies above?
- Pay attention to details; not drama.
- That moment when one question can bring about a serious self-reflection and revelation.
- If you see an abyss and have to run towards it, that means you can't show restraint, then you are a slave to your own weaknesses. Don't give in. just because you're hungry doesn't mean you give in to food all the time. Just because you can do something does not mean it's good for you or will benefit you. Let's live and learn. Learn to live better.
- Predestination, so does our destiny choose us?
- It's nice to give thanks to the moment, in order to appreciate the future. Don't be fooled, if you can't appreciate anything about your current situation, no matter how bad, how can you appreciate your present circumstance as a road to progress.
- What's going on? There is so much to hate in the world, with so little to love, so much to hope for, but so little to hold on to. So much uncertainty, compounded with insecurity. People have lost faith in humanity, and they should, even our leaders have lost hope and are clueless on how to deal with global crisis.

- Beauty is seen and instantly the moment of recognition that clouds reasoning is given birth to, and puts you in a state of awe and appreciation, but all for different reasons – it could be appreciating a work of Art, a person or place. It's not always skin deep or superficial.

- Don't be fooled, good people do bad things and bad folks can be affiliated with good things too. How do we make sense of this? Some intentionally go out of their way to do bad things, while others do bad things unintentionally. Those that fall under the unintentional, get remorseful with time, and see the errors of their ways; the others don't. and so on and so forth.

- Only the bold dare Stand Alone. There Is Not Always Comfort in Numbers. Don't Be Afraid to Fly Alone.

- No matter how pressed your goals or desires are, sometimes life throws issues at you that make preferences over your "so called priority". For instance those fleeing war zones are not thinking about their bills or love difficulties, but "survival". That has become their only goal to survive, not conform.

- Hmmm. It amazes me how folks are shocked by honesty, but are numb to lies and deceit.

- Just because something isn't a lie does not mean that it isn't deceptive. A liar knows that he is a liar, but one who speaks mere portions of truth in order to deceive is a craftsman of destruction.

- If you are having trouble focusing now and then, it's completely natural and there are simple things you can do to get through it. But if you find yourself frequently unengaged which, to be honest, is also quite common, the solution is going to take a bit more thought.

- A child being carried at the back of his mother does not know how long the journey is (Nigerian adage).
- When did tacky become the new "sexy" or "hot". A lady can be covered all over and still be desirable. What's this worldly craze or race to bare all? A lady or man that is sure of themselves can wear anything and come out on top. Looking good is not leaving anything to the imagination, it just shows how much value you place on yourself, and that same value will be placed upon you by those that are interested.
- Don't be fooled; sometimes those that pretend they don't care…care the most. A lot who take time to save or help others, need saving or help themselves.
- What's the essence of our daily life battles and struggles? Or is the struggle the essence? Does the moulding of our core being lay in the struggle? Is it through the pain, we appreciate peace? Is through togetherness we appreciate our own presence? Is through singleness that we appreciate togetherness?
- Identity crisis: Identity is who you are, what you represent, what you uphold. Belief, etc. nowadays, with this crisis, it's hard to identify who anybody really is. People hiding in the shadows about who they REALLY are, yet speaking and representing another belief out in public. Some will copy everything about you or others, including hobbies, some think through you or others, and indirectly live their lives not being theirs. You might as well

not have a brain. It's better for someone to have an identity, no matter how disagreeable it is, than someone who does not. Folks will rather be seen "belonging" or "fitting in" than a unique individual we are. This could boil down to a lot of things i.e. insecurity, no self-belief, no entelechy, one who has no direction, no sense of belonging, no principles, or satisfaction and psychological issues, etc.

- Sometimes what you are running away from is what you are running towards.

- Being indecisive or too complacent can be self-destructive. Progress in anything then becomes mute or stagnant, just because you can't make up your mind. Make a decision and stand by it. If later on it doesn't work, then there is no crime in changing, refocusing or redefining.

- Assert your own personality without robbing someone of theirs. Always give "You" to the world, as we already have enough people cloning other personalities, just to conform. Why supress you? You maybe what the world just needs.

- The perception of anything is never the reality of anything.

- We all have priorities, but life can throw obstacles that make way to "preference" over priority. No matter how principled we are, there comes a time when principled opposition needs to give pre-eminence or way for the greater good.

- Am I the only one thinking all these known nuclear testing and secret underwater/ground nuclear testing could have impinged these furious hurricanes. I don't think these are "Natural disasters", but "Man-made disasters"…Just a thought. PS: I stand corrected if anyone can prove otherwise.

- Evil does not act itself, it always has willing and premeditated participants.
- Some people find an excuse not to do anything. Why change, when you have ready-made excuses?
- Sometimes you may trust someone, but not trust the situation they surround or put themselves in.
- I'm a single guy with a complex nature.
- Only a fool gets attached to their own pain and is led by it.
- Beautiful faces are in vogue, but beautiful minds are sure hard to find.
- Don't fool yourself about the ones that never talk because they eventually will, but will they listen or understand?
- So ironic: it's hard to be open minded in a world full of closed minds. It's hard to be lateral in your views when most will rather be medial. It's hard to trust because everyone is already suspicious, even when there is no reason to be. It's hard to call out useless politicians or fake preachers when the majority want to aspire to be them. It's hard to call out the hypocrites because it's the norm today, so most feel at home. A world where most are incorrigible, but to conform is the order of the day. Damn, I feel so isolated for the right reasons.
- Incredible how terrorists are caught within days, but alarming how they hardly solve mere burglaries.

AM I missing something? The answer sure lays in-between.

- Don't be fooled, chaos brings about security for some twisted political agendas. While the masses are distracted with frivolous matters, devious and self-interest political aims are achievable.
- The mystical essence of spirituality is; Priceless.
- Good memories will always have the pre-eminence over bad ones. Although, the choice to let either rule you, is up to you.
- Have you been lied too? Well, that can be redeemed, but if you have been lying to yourself…hmmm. You only heap and procrastinate dire consequences on you. The mask you wear haunts you.
- It's wise to know what you're eating before you get fed up. Why build up such anticipation just to be disappointed?
- Why do folks pay more attention to 'what you didn't say', rather than what you are saying?

LOVE NUGGETS

- When you have too many walls up in your nature, that nobody can feel free around you or you don't let anybody in, you hinder your soul from connecting to others and blossoming.
- Some love the idea of being in love, but are detached from the reality of staying in love. It is one thing to want it. It's another thing to be ready.
- Let no corrupt communication proceed out of your mouth, but that which is good to the use of edifying, that it may minister/impact grace unto the hearers…The Word undiluted for those of you judgemental people, preaching fire and brimstone. Get it right, and start concentrating and preaching 'love', and don't concern yourself with what people are or are not doing.
- ENTWINE: Once in a lifetime, someone will appear in your life and make a positive, yet sensual effect on your life, and all effort to deny that become cul-de-sac. When, how and why become fruitless? I guess it boils down to "it was just meant to be". The hold one person can have on you becomes almost mystical, then your life is on a stand still all of a sudden, and nothing seems to make sense…hmmm. The relationship then takes you on a rollercoaster, that can either crash or lead to bliss. You see that person as one with you in every single aspect.
- A great gift, requires a great sacrifice to man, but LOVE gives life without any sacrifice required, because love paid the ultimate price.

- You never know the impact a hug can have, until you are in direct need of one. The little things have the most significant effect.
- The moments in Life that take your breath away, hold more substance than just existing. Always freeze those cherish able moments, as they come handy in difficult times, and will always bring a smile to your heart.
- Love blossoms and can give raise to warm feelings, but when it withers, resentment takes over, if you embrace it.
- How come the best love songs are written out of a place of hurt?
- True love gives your heart a brand new song…. who's singing?
- When you find that 'one person' that makes you feel like you are home, even a warrior, will hesitate at his choices for her because she sure makes you smile with your heart. As a good woman will always bring out the best in him, and the weakest in him simultaneously.
- Loving people unconditionally, scares people. The thought of entertaining it, makes us flinch in disapproval. Not because it's wrong, but because it's a reflection of our boundaries. It testifies to our limitations of the "so called Love". We claim to have. In reality, we "accept" initially, with a hidden notion to "change" later on down the road, especially, in regard to relationships. This applies a lot to women, although a few men do the same. Do we even know how to love unconditionally?

- While absence and distance make the heart fonder, jealousy can make the mind wonder.

RELATIONSHIPS NUGGETS

- I guess I was so blinded by who I wanted you to be, that I didn't see who you really are.
- Some friends and couples hate each other. Not because they are full of hate, but simply because they fail to understand each other.
- Friendship built on common grounds only will end up in a brink of disaster someday. Tolerance of indifference stands the test of time.
- Working on any relationship starts with working on yourself and not working on the other party to change.
- When conflict in any relationship is seen as a misunderstanding, then a true relationship has arisen.
- Everything in a relationship is easy, only if you detach yourself from it. Otherwise it's continuous work and redefining.
- Sometimes we have to see past the pain hurt and bitterness that we possess, in order to see the good in another. If not, all your decisions, motives and progress will be based and driven by hurt, etc.
- Human emotions are far from 'Taps' – like where you can choose hot or cold water. Emotions and consequences of the relationship still remain. Now how you deal with the aftermath shows wisdom, maturity or foolishness.

- Those that love obsessively also destroy obsessively. Their obsession eventually turns compulsive.
- The decline of moral values has a knock- on effect on the modern day approach to relationships. The greed and race to be self-sufficient and "look out for self" and "what can I get out of it" is fast taking over the need to focus on what's best for the relationship as partners.
- Your relationship doesn't need to make sense to anyone, except you and your partner. It's a relationship, not a community project.
- Don't be blinded by who you want someone to be that you then lose or fail to see who they really are.
- Having a jealous partner that needs no reason to accuse you of anything can limit or threaten your free will to be. No matter how much you assure them, their jealous nature will always outweigh your reassurance.
- Lovers don't find each other…souls do.
- Unresolved emotions, intentionally or unintentionally, are a recipe for disaster and hinders any kind of relationship. It stunts any spiritual or mental growth.
- It takes a second for a lack of humour to suck the romance out of a relationship.
- Don't be fooled, everything you admire or envy in a person could be a lie, façade or a fragment of your own built up imagination about an individual or individuals. Some folks don't even consider this

notion, not in the slightest, as the mind is mostly carried away with what is 'felt' and 'seen' than what we 'know'. What you 'think' you know about anyone that you are not close to is merely a shot in the dark, and a shot in the dark hardly meets its target.

THE WORD NUGGETS

- I have been young, and now am old; yet have I not seen the righteous forsaken nor his seed begging for bread.
- The Lord is my strength and song, and has become my salvation; He is my God and I will prepare Him a habitation, my father's God, and I will exalt him.
- His heart is upheld, he will not fear; until he looks with satisfaction on his adversaries.
- He stores up wisdom for the upright; He is a shield to those who walk in integrity.
- He keepeth all his bones; not one of them is broken.
- Praying always with all prayer and supplication in the spirit.
- Is not my Word like as a fire? saith the Lord; and like a hammer that breaketh the rock in pieces?
- Love is patient, love is kind. It does not envy, it does not boast, it is not proud. It is not rude, it is not self-seeking. It is not easily angered, it keeps no record of wrongs. Love does not delight in evil but rejoices with the truth. It always protects, always trusts, always hopes, always perseveres. Is that you? Sure not. Love is God; God is love.
- The Word: If any of you lack wisdom, let him ask of God, that giveth to all men liberally, and upbraideth not; and it shall be given him; but let him ask in faith, nothing wavering. For he that wavereth is like a wave of the sea driven with the wind and tossed… Emphasis on "Wavereth". Don't waver in

anything, especially when you ask. He who wavers, doubts.

- “For my thoughts are not your thoughts, neither are your ways my ways”, declares the Lord, “As the heavens are higher than the earth, so are my ways higher than your ways and my thoughts than your thoughts.
- Say to wisdom, “You are my sister”, and call understanding your intimate friend.
- It is better not to make a vow, than make one and not fulfil it.
- Attaching importance to anything does not mean you have control over the situation. Neither does it mean you fully understand the situation. Don’t be fooled, even when you think you are in “control”, it’s only temporary. Control of anything, is in the hands of He who holds your time.
- Whoever looks for good, will find kindness.
- If those that teach you say, ‘The Kingdom of God’ is in the sky, then the birds of the sky will precede you. If they say, it is in the sea, then the fish will precede you. Know this: The Kingdom is inside of you and around you. Only a few see it around them.

WISDOM NUGGETS

- Facts don't normally cooperate with the truth. This in no way makes it less true. Note: not all truths have proven answers.
- Stop clinging onto hate. Hate has a funny way of poisoning human blood and infecting the mind. Hate consumes slowly and like a virus, takes over your nature. Eventually it clouds your judgement and controls your thought. Stop being ruled by it. What a sad way to live.
- Deep thinking is far from over thinking. Over thinking does not change a situation and can be harmful, and borderline, giving a depressive state of mind.
- What you know does not stop you from being who you are.
- Wisdom of a profound mind is, when you realise that we control nothing, even when we are in control.
- There is no greater aphrodisiac than one who has "a mind" of their own. One who is never afraid to swift through influence of others, but add their own thoughts, spin and conclusion on relative and unrelated issues. It's refreshing being 'you'. Don't be fooled 'fakeness' is smelt a mile away.
- The nature of a promise or vow is that it remains immune to natural or changing circumstances. Think twice before you commit to anything.

- Guilt is an enormous burden to carry. It can rule the way you manoeuvre, if you let it. The quantum of guilt outweighs the deed in most cases. This in turn brings about a crisis of conscience that mentally paralyses the guilty party, controls the mind and taints the soul. Again, only if you cooperate with 'Guilt'. But to control guilt is understanding that God outweighs the deed. Release that guilty burden unto He that holds your time, that peace may reign.
- Indifference or a misunderstanding should not turn you ugly.
- No matter where you get it from, always listen to the voice of reason.
- Some folks feed off listening to your problems, not because they care at all and are not listening to understand or care either. Careful who you whisper your problems to.
- Diseases have a cause not motive. People have the latter.
- It is nice to learn from the wise and forget folks that act "otherwise".
- All it takes is one incident to redefine you and bring a thin line between you being confident, and being vulnerable. Being vulnerable does not mean you are weak either.
- Never ask a drunk person, what they really think about you.
- You can't imagine how deep pain runs; sharper than a thousand knives, and in some cases, it's buried deep within the person involved. So deep, some

folks don't talk about it but Memories are not easily erased and actions give a glimmer of what lies deep within. It is better to confront and not bury it. Nevertheless, be careful who you whisper the most sacred parts of you to, let them earn your trust and not just because they say you can trust them. Apply wisdom when looking for solutions to past issues. Not everyone that gives their ears, gives their heart…Just a thought.

- The worst thing that can happen to you is not being true to yourself. Stop living for how others view you. Why grow old before your time?
- What does the age of Methuselah (oldest living man), have to do with the wisdom of Solomon? In short, what does ones age have to do with the way they apply wisdom, knowledge and understanding to anything? Age does not automatically give you this, hence the Word…'Out of the mouths of babes and suckling hast thou ordained strength'.
- Dealing with stupidity can be life threatening, just when you think they can't get any stupider, there they go again…Better to just ignore and give yourself some peace.
- Never define anyone by their worst moments.
- I see this a lot, and it is scary for any individual man or woman to be indecisive. A simple decision now lingers into a month. There are a million things to make decisions on, but you become mute, and progress lingers in all dimensions. Creativity is the act of making the possible practical, but there is nothing practical about being indecisive. Just think

and make a decision and relieve yourself of this indecisive burden.

- Think hard and be well informed before you accuse folks publicly of anything.

- Yes, we have to respect people's views but that does not mean you have to honour or condone their views.

- Never let your comfort zone be your worst enemy. Never let your comfort zone limit you. Let your spirit set you free. You are more than your boundaries. Your inner spirit is limitless, and cannot be contained by your flesh, unless you continue to cage it.

- It is a moral and spiritual crime to be jobless and content, idle and itchy. Life is not easy for anyone but at least put in cffort. Before you become a nuisance unto yourself and others.

- Never put your eggs in one basket, they say. But what if life throws one available choice or basket, for argument sake, at you. Do you discard the basket? Some risks are worth taking until other doors present itself. As long as the basket or risk does not compromise your principles and is not detrimental to your health, go for it. That basket might turn itself into other baskets in due time.

- The beauty of life takes a while to find and chaos can be a great catalyst.

- Stop hanging around people who give excuses not to be with you, a million others will appreciate your time more.

- Thanking God for a Miracle of me. Yes, we are walking miracles in every sense. Don't go chasing false miracles only in regard to money. Rise above that.
- There is nothing like a man and woman that exudes knowledge and shares hers or his wisdom. Now, that's a giver of Life that builds nations and is sure worth listening to.
- There is nothing wrong in having high standards or expectations, but if this is wrapped up in low self-esteem, coupled with disproportionately high and deluded expectations, then you are simply throwing yourself back in a whirlwind and driven by an alter ego. If you fall into this group, then it's time you ask yourself different questions, step back and learn to rid yourself of unrealistic expectations. Nevertheless, there's nothing wrong in having big dreams, but not big egos.
- Perseverance adds usefulness to patience, but that does not necessarily mean you're a patient person, even though patience and perseverance are intertwined. Some circumstances demand your patience; when it is forced, your being patient, as anything else, will be a catastrophe. Even the impatient can be forced to be patient in life changing circumstances.
- There is no greater truth than being truthful to those around you. Although the latest trend is to hang around folks that feed your negative lifestyle.
- I guess only a fool will choke on wise words without digesting them.
- More is lost by indecision than by wrong decisions.

- The Mind of a Man; Who can contain it…adheres to Wisdom. The Spirit of a Man, rises above you.
- Sometimes the little you have is the best you'll ever have. You just refused to see and understand it.
- Always lend an ear to an artist that sings from a place of hurt and recovery. There's always a message to identify with or learn from it.
- The secrets of Man shall be judged…If this does not create fear of God in you, then I don't know what will.
- Do we really give into our True phenomenal nature or just adapt to flesh? Our full potential seems to be masked by our bodies, giving into the flesh. Whilst our full potential lay silently within, waiting to be tapped into, and bursting with mystery. Some of us will dic, not cvcn knowing we possess such phenomenal talent. A lot of gold we seek, lay within us.
- I've realised in Life, you are as good as you're able; Able to drive; Able to eat; Able to work; Able to see; Able to hear; Able to breathe; Able to walk; All the "Ables". Stop believing your own Hype. Be humble.
- In life, I have learnt that what you ask for is what you normally should expect and deserve. But what you expect and what you get are sometimes worlds apart. The worst kind of expectations are the unrealistic ones. Learn to give room to bumpy roads during your expectations, for how can one win a war, if you are not expecting it.

- A lot of misplaced direction and appreciation comes from "what have I achieved", than "what have I enjoyed" or enjoying. It's nice to give thanks to the moment, in order to appreciate the future.
- In life, what you see is not what you get, and what you get, is not in most cases, what you expected. Try being content, it normally removes the element of surprise and suspense. Seeing is sure not believing.
- Sudden life changing issues don't test your patience, but your ability to adjust.
- Do we hang around people that influence us positively or people that feed our bad habits?
- Sometimes we do things, not because they are easy or possible, but because they are necessary.
- When looking for advice, never speak to the wrong people, and expect to get the right answers.
- When you shake a tree hard enough, something is bound to fall off. Whether what you find is relevant or not, is another thing. Whether you are prepared for your discovery or answer, is another thing too. Before you rock a boat, ask yourself if you are ready for the consequences and not just the drama.
- The truth does not mean you abide by it. It simply is the truth, irrespective of freewill.
- Being blind is not just about what you can't see, but mostly what you don't understand.
- Being down once in a while is OK, but being defeated has dire consequences.

- Truth seeking requires us to grow beyond our limited means. To know the truth is to seek it with persistence, curiosity and humility.

- Making sense does not equal making progress, although progress is relative, as in some cases you have to be stagnant in order for progress to rear its head. Love, progress or success, but don't be obsessed with it, least it ruin you.

- When you look at many faces for too long; when you pay attention, with a little patience. You are bound to see the many faces of "Man" living in "one body". Truth is, all the faces are one person – both the good and bad. Until we master how to deal with, and understand the bad or difficult persona of "Man", our limited and ignorant perception will continue to prevail over our physical beings.

- Greed is fast becoming a motivator in ladies hooking up with men or vice versa. A lot can sniff money from afar, and will snatch a man from his wife or vice versa. Have you heard of "look before you leap"? It's always easy for a man to spend money during an affair, but what's in it for you? Do you know the source of his money? Do you know if the wife is the breadwinner and he is spending her money or their savings to impress you? Some only realise this when they are pregnant and the flow of money miraculously becomes dry. Be your own person and source of inspiration. Stop trying to reap where another woman has sown, just because it looks good from the outside. Stop envying ready made because change can come to any man or woman. Independence is not taking from another, but building.

- If love and hate are two horns on the same goat, both feelings come from within, showing us that the ability to make or destroy ourselves lies within us. Emotions control both sources and your ability to choose which one rules you is where reason, which also lays within you, comes in. Which switch are you controlled by? Hate, love, jealousy, insecurity, etc. you have the ability to turn that source off.
- Do not spoil what you have by desiring what you have not. Remember, that which you now have was once among the things you only hoped for.
- Don't be fooled, owing someone an explanation does not mean you owe them an apology.
- Finish each day and be done with it. You have done what you could. Some blunders and absurdities, no doubt, crept in; forget them as soon as you can because tomorrow is a new day. Sift out the negative words and those who feed off drama. Don't be consumed with "what if's", but "what is". You and only you can turn a new leaf and shall begin it serenely and with too high a spirit to be encumbered with your old nonsense.
- A strong woman is full of accomplishment, not attitude. She weathers the strongest storms, yet never gives up or moans. She uses her time wisely and "owns" her mistakes, instead of blaming men or the world for her troubles. She refrains from bitterness. She embraces all. She shields her worries. She is secure in herself and her intuition gets the best of her. She does not pride herself with fake compliments and least of all does not confuse her strong attributes with attitude.

- Whatever is taken for granted will eventually be taken away. Instead of complaining about what you want, try to enjoy what you have.
- Beware of those who don't respect personal boundaries. Don't be fooled by thinking they are oblivious to their actions because they are fully aware of this. It's just a total disregard to your nature because it's all about them.
- Sometimes in life, you need to ask questions, and in some cases you are forced to question, but you should question anyway, until you get an answer that makes sense or that you can't argue with.
- To love a tree and hate its fruit is like loving God, but rejecting the gateway He provides to salvation.
- You can't change what life throws at you, but you can changc how it affects you. You can change how you react to it; how it defines you. We do make the mistake of taking it out on those that are close to us. God help us and give us courage to rise above our life issues.
- Stop trying to say, "Something is wrong", without saying something is wrong, unless you don't want a resolution; as prolonged anxiety only eats away valuable time.
- Only an unprincipled person will degrade themselves just to prove a point.
- Curiosity is a catalyst to knowledge, but not in regard to boundaries that invade people's private affairs. Everyone has a lane to stay in, but for those that carelessly derail...Remember, if you fly too close to the sun, you will surely get burnt.

- Truth seeking about anything in life requires us to grow beyond our limited means. To know the truth is to seek it with persistence, curiosity and humility.
- What do you do for a living? We normally ask, but how about what we live for? I think it's more profound.
- Hidden stress has a way of resurfacing. Don't hide it, least you feed it. Talk to someone.
- Devote yourself to perfection of whatever you pursue. Have breaks, if you can, slowly but surely things have a way of falling into place. Devote yourself utterly to a set of moral principles. Seek the stillness of your mind and soul. Be disciplined and principled in your quest for discovery. Always ask, crave and walk towards peace and tranquillity. Rebel only against untruths and conformity.
- I rely on no man or "Man of God" and I will continue to test all spirits, and "doctrines of man" with the brain that God gave me, with no fear and without prejudice. A perfect man answered all questions in Christ, so show yourselves approved as Christ did or move. I'm not a "feel good" or emotional Christian, as that's what breeds cultism, brain washing and mental slavery.
- When is sorry not enough? Are you sorry for what you did? If so, then it should be enough. Or are you just sorry that you were caught? Not enough. Your act here is probably being malicious and premeditated. Let your sorry hold substance, or don't to utter the words.
- When you are indecisive in all ramifications, progress lingers in all dimensions.

- Don't be over righteous. Why destroy yourself?
- Only a fool lies all the time and does not have the decency, to have a good memory.
- Stop saying a lot less than you mean to, even though you mean to say a lot more. Say it or don't, as in-between does not cut it.
- Never underestimate the power of silence.
- It's easy to hurt people, but it's wiser to think of the consequences of our actions. Learn this or Karma will teach you.
- Time out for Reflection…Priceless.
- Time decides who you want in your life, and your behaviour decides who stays in your life.
- Sometimes the only victory you need is over your own self-doubt.
- Beware of those who don't respect personal boundaries. Don't be fooled by thinking they are oblivious to their actions because they are fully aware of this. It's just a total disregard to your nature because it's all about them.
- Thanking God for the miracle of me. Thank God for the miracle of my children. Thank God for the miracle of my siblings. Thank God for the miracle of my friends, loved ones and well-wishers on Facebook. Yes, we are walking miracles in every sense. Stop mocking God with false and superficial miracles only in regard to money and you. Rise above that.

- God sees the heart, not what you present to the world.
- Sometimes the best you can do is use the resources available to you. Sometimes the best thing to do is Nothing.
- Don't be fooled, even the nicest of people can harbour the deadliest and most shocking secrets.
- Don't ever live your life like it's one big fat never ending party, because in reality, parties end and the reality you left behind will be waiting in the oven for you. Staring you right back in the face. Yes, we all need an outlet to let our hair down once in a while, but only a fool takes his eye off the ball. When the music of the party stops, don't let reality flood your future with misery and emptiness. A touch of reality.
- Why focus too much on enemies? A lot of them are born out of the consequences of our actions, right or wrong anyway, and sometimes not. It's not our place to focus on them and miss the big picture. Most will direct you where you need to be anyway (if only they knew…lol). Remember you are someone's enemy also, intentionally or not. Leave your worries and enemies to He who answereth by Fire.
- Only a fool gets attached to their own pain and is led by it. The choice to be free or caged by it is yours.
- Start by making sense of any mess or madness you are in. Clarity is progress.

- Talk all you want, as long as you understand or can defend what you talk about. Be informed.

- Difficulties test courage, patience, perseverance and true character of a human being. Adversity and hardship make a person strong and ready to face the challenges of life with equanimity. There is no doubt that there can be no gain without pain. It is only when one toils and sweats it out that success is nourished, respected and sustained. Success attained otherwise, like an inheritance is not a test of success.

- Sometimes we have heard things more than we know them. Sometimes we have heard, read and are familiar with a name or thing, more than we understand too. Be better informed. Be cautious of your findings. Be aware of your limitations, but never limit yourself. A form of knowledge can be very deceitful.

- Sometimes you have to forget all you think you know or learnt and just pay attention.

www.ingramcontent.com/pod-product-compliance
Ingram Content Group UK Ltd.
Pitfield, Milton Keynes, MK11 3LW, UK
UKHW042000190726
13854UKWH00005B/2094